I0469671

Table of Contents

Copyright 2013

All About Drop Shippers

The small business has a problem when they first start their business with finding a reasonable priced storage place. It is necessary to have a place to keep product stored until ready to put them in your retail outlet. This is expensive and a waste of space. That is why the sudden boom in having an online store. A small businessperson can set up their store from home and monitor it from home. The profit margin can be very high depending on the amount of time you spend searching for the right product and the right drop shipper. The right drop shipper is everything in the virtual online store.

The drop shipper helps you to get rid of all the issues that slow you down and cost you money. The advantages of using the right drop shipper can make or break your business. The following is a brief description of the advantages you as a business owner benefit by using a good drop shipper.

> ➤ First drop shippers do the research for products and provide you with their lists and catalogues of available items at trade prices. It is up to you to sell any of these items by any method you wish.
> ➤ You make the sell and receive payment before the drop shipper fulfills the order.
> ➤ Drop shippers package your orders so you never have to package an order again.
> ➤ Drop shippers send your orders out to your customers saving you a trip to the post office plus your name and address is on the product.

- ➢ Since your name and address is on the product, the drop shipper becomes invisible to your customers leaving you as the only person for them to contact.
- ➢ Drop shippers hold the entire product so you do not have to lay out many cash for product. You can spend your full focus on marketing and taking the money to the bank.

These are just some of the advantages of working with a drop shipper. The more reputable drop shippers offer you online help, your own web site and to a degree will advise you of the on going products that are hot in the market for today's sales. Remember in today's world product changes often as does the consumers need for the product. That is why it is very important that you work with a reputable drop shipper that can help you to keep a breast of what is going on today and what tomorrow looks like.

The drop shipper is the heartbeat of your company. Remember in order to maintain a good standing all the way round keep informed and up to date on all that is happening in the wholesale market. Use good senses when selecting a drop shipper to avoid fraud and misleading your customer do research on the different companies that offer the service. When you find the company, you are satisfied with then it is best to stick with the company you trust. The drop shipper is more than glad to let you know their ratings and the BBB will inform you of their business practice. The BBB is a good place to start your research on a drop shipper that you feel will fulfill your needs for your business. You should have in mind the types of products that you want to sell and how you want to handle your company then selecting the drop shipper will be a lot easier.

Drop Shipping

For many years businesses have use Drop Shipping as a means to move merchandise to customers. It has become very popular especially with small business. It is one of the tools that business uses to enlarge the staff and to enhance the service. It also saves overhead expenses it saves gas and it saves time.

It just makes good sense if you are selling online, and especially if you are the only in your business, to use a drop shipper. When you use a drop shipper you have a larger inventory to offer your customers. Most companies do not have large warehouses to store merchandise even more so most companies cannot afford to rent or own a large storage facility. Many companies operate from one room in the home and use drop shipping to extend the company facilities. It is a very simple process if you want to use a drop shipper to help you move your merchandise. Some businesses have become a success because they have used Drop Shipping to enhance their business. When you are using drop shipping as a means to move your merchandise or to send orders you really don't have to leave your home.

All can be done from your computer or even a mail order catalog. Most homes today have computers and use them to sell merchandise online. All you have to do is send the wholesale cost of the merchandise to your drop shipper and the name and address of your customer and the Drop Shipping company will send your merchandise right to your customer's door. This saves you a lot of time because you don't have to address labels you don't have to wrap packages and then go to the post office. You may stay at home and do all of this from your desk. It is much more convenient to Drop Ship when you are getting your merchandise from the same company that is doing the Drop

Shipping. Check with your drop shipper and become very familiar with the rules and regulations of the company. In many instances you can save money if you order larger quantities of goods from the company. This sometimes depends on whether you are Drop Shipping retail or whether you are Drop Shipping wholesale. There are many companies who sell both retail and wholesale and will Drop Ship for both. Perhaps the most important thing you need to know before you start Drop Shipping is policies of the company.

The company policies will let you know what you can do and what you can not do. One thing you need to consider is what you will do with the merchandise if it is returned. Some Drop Ship companies will not allow you to return merchandise. Some companies who offer to do Drop Shipping will sale return merchandise locally. Don't forget to check out the Drop Shipper's reputation; in addition find out how long the company has been in business. When a company has been in business for a while you will know it by the way he does business. If you are in doubt about a company you are considering you can check with the Better Business Bureau.

Shipping

Shipping is one of the most aspects of any business whether it is a retail outlet or an online virtual storefront. The cost of shipping can make a deep cut into the profit margin.

Most small business owners try to find the best way to ship at the lowest prices. Small businesses depend on drop shippers with the product in order to save on their bottom line. That is one of the best ways of saving the business expense without to much hassle. The customer may not always buy a product that is dropped shipped instead you might be packaging up the product and hurry off to a good shipper. When you buy in lots normally, the whole unit comes to you personally. When you then put it on eBay or your own web site then you will need to find a way to ship to the consumer.

The number one most accepted shipper is the United States Post Office. The US Post Office is prompt and uses great care in handling packages. Shipping has become such a big business that the post office now provides the supplies you need, pick up and delivery as well as over night delivery. The post office tracking system is simple going on line, put in your receipt number, and find out the exact time and date of delivery. You can also insure your product if it has a value that would be considered a loss. You can also keep a postal machine in your office that you can use to calculate the postage and print the postage necessary. The United States Post Office is one of our better methods of shipping.

Shipping via Ups is also a great way to go especially if you happen to have larger packages or boxes. Ups offers access quantum view, which is a method for you to keep up with your clients. You can maintain a database and track their deliveries etc. Remember for those who sell to retail outlets a product that is repeatedly on a weekly or monthly basis Ups is an excellent way to go. You will get automatic pickup service and you can track delivery as well as shortages etc. Ups will go to the manufacturer pick up the product for you and then deliver to your customer. This is an excellent way for you to buy in quantity and ship. Someone has to pay for the shipping and that is where you really have to watch out the cost. The cost can really eat into your profits. You might be able to charge it to the client or at least split the cost 50/50 in any case this would help your bottom line.

Large products like furniture for instances is best shipped via a semi and one of the best company's with the best rates is Yellow Truck. You can access the company on line and track your shipment the same way as you do with Ups and the United States Post Office. All manner of shipping is important so that you can maintain a profitable business.

Drop Shippers and You

Are you looking for a stay at home business that you can earn enough money for yourself and your family? You have heard so much about people who have sold on eBay and made a bundle but you are afraid that you might invest and loose. There are the stories and nightmares told by those who have also lost their shirt. You cannot afford to do this but you feel that you must do something as your company is closing and moving out of the country. What a dilemma for anyone to be involved.

Drop Shippers and Distributors have approached you with emails and the like trying to get you to invest in their sure fire business. That they guarantee that you cannot loose is no comfort because you have no backup proof of their existence. The problem even though they give you this promise you have no way of knowing how reliable this Drop Shipper maybe. What does a drop shipper have to offer that will help you in your business adventure? What am I to look for when trying to select a good drop shipper? It has been said that about 90% of business people go out of business not because of lack of effort or a good business plan but because they were misinformed. Lack of information is the killer to almost all business. Just like traveling, you should have a GP Tracker or at least a road map.

That is why a Wholesale & Drop Shipper catalog was created for those who are new in business and for those who are very active in business. If your plans are to remain in this business you need to keep up to date at all times. One thing for sure you must know what is going on at all times keeping up with the hottest of products. The catalog is your road map to good business health. The Distributor has also become the drop shipper now that the advent of a virtual shop on the web has made it possible for anyone to set up shop.

The drop shipper has become a virtual Angel for anyone who wishes to set up business with little or no money. The drop shipper provides the product and delivery method with no cost to you. You just maintain your store and do the marketing while the drop shipper provides the product and delivery.

There are various ways that you can sell products and use a drop shipper to help you with storing the product and delivery of the product. One way to earn money on line is to join an Affiliate Program where many manufacturers will give you a cut of the profits on products that you sell for them. Sell your products on eBay it requires no more than a computer. Once you become an active trader, you can ease into a Website by opening up your own eBay store. You can use Google's AdSense to put an ad that is relevant to your website when a visitor clicks on the ad they automatically go to your site. Remember to sell drop ship products in order to keep your expenses down and the product quality up.

Wholesale Drop Shipping

Wholesale Drop Shipping has become a booming business. This business is global in nature because everywhere in the world there is some Drop Shipping taking place. It is a very simple process that retail businesses enjoy using. The wholesale Drop Shipping business has one primary function and that is to move merchandise from warehouse to customer for the retail businesses. Because of this wholesale Drop Shipping business, people all over the world can enjoy merchandise from any other part of the world. Before the start of wholesale Drop Shipping, the same merchandise was shipped by the wholesaler and again by the retailer before the customer received it.

In other words, the retail company used to order from the wholesale and then have to ship to the customer. With the use of wholesale Drop Shipping service the retailer can simply send the name and other customer information to the Drop Shipping company and the wholesale Drop Shipping company will send the merchandise directly to the custom. Drop Shipping has become as common as going to the post office. Profit by the retailer is made on the difference between the wholesale price and the retail price. Every other company at one time or another uses a Drop Shipping company to deliver goods to a customer. The Drop Shipping business has helped many small business owners to stay afloat. The expenses of a company are considerably less when Drop Shippers are used.

The complete shipping process for the retailer is modified and the wholesale Drop Shipper redefines the shipping process. Many jobs have been reclassified because of Drop Shipping. Some personnel have found it necessary to do other jobs than what they have been accustom to doing.

Just about every other business uses a Drop Shipper to move merchandise to customers. If you have an online business or a catalog business Drop Shipping is one of the best way to get merchandise to your customer. Drop Shipping is easy and a friendly process that can be used and enjoyed by all businesses. Drop Shipping has enhanced the bottom-line for many large and small businesses. The two most important things that Drop Shipping helps the retailer with are, it cuts down on paperwork and it cuts out the shipping steps.

With wholesale Drop Shipping a whole new world economy has become available. The retailer can find customers all over the world any items anywhere in the world that you may have a need for or a desire for can be found online and Drop Shipped to you. What ever you wish to sell can be found in one form or another through the wholesale Drop Shipping process. Drop Shipping has become a quick and easy way to get started in e-commerce. Two other advantages of Drop Shipping are in the case of a small business no money is invested up front; and the second advantage is that there is no danger of having unsold merchandise in you inventory. After all when you use the Drop Shipping methods you purchase merchandise only when you have sold merchandise. Therefore you do not have to worry about an oversupply of one item and an undersupply of another item when you go the wholesale Drop Shipping way.

Drop Shipping Helps Business

Drop Shipping can add to the bottom line of any business large or small. Many businesses thrive off of Drop Shipping because it cuts down on their overhead. Services can be cut out and staff also when a business is Drop Shipping. For that reason, businesses find it economical to Drop Ship to most of their customers. Drop Shipping gives businesses flexibility in their day to day operations. A limited number of staff members can be used to get a large volume of work done. This adds to the bottom line at the end of a year.

Drop Shipping also cuts down on staff training and orientation. There is no need to train personnel how to ship merchandise when a Drop Shipper is used. If it is proprietorship business, and the proprietor works from home, there is a tremendous savings in the gas bill alone. One room in the home can be set up to operate a successful business if a Drop Shipper is used. So there is no need to buy furniture and expensive equipment. The average home operation can survive and thrive off of a few pieces of office equipment.

The computer is one of those pieces of equipment that is a must have for the average small home business. In addition in order to Drop Ship it becomes necessary in many instances to have access to a fax machine. And of course you must have ma bell to call your Drop Ship company from time to time and your customers. Most of the Drop Ship companies that have been in business for a while and know their way around will give you a quick turnaround on all of you orders. When you use a Drop Ship company there is no competition fold good-quality help. When you compete for help that increases your expenses because good help has to be paid a decent salary and you have to factor in benefits such as insurance, sick leave and paid vacations. Drop shipping is a wonderful tool for small businesses with limited staff and limited resources. For many businesses it is hard to see a difference between expenses and income that equals profit. So choosing a Drop Ship company is of uttermost importance.

After all businesses are in business to make a profit. But by using a Drop Ship company, the chances of making a profit is more of a reality. When you factor in all of the benefits that have been deleted by using a Drop Ship company and all of the expenses saved by working out of your home, chances are great that you will have success in your business. Drop shipping is a great way to cut corners when you are in business. You don't even have to keep up with the changes in shipping rates and rules and regulations. We all know that they are constantly changing especially since the 911 event. Drop Shipping helps a business to become more efficient and gives the customer a quicker turnaround. All customers want a quick turnaround when an order is placed you sometimes start looking for the item the very next day or two after the order has been placed. Drop shipping gives one of the fastest turnaround of all methods of ordering and shipping. Let's face it they have the tools and the necessary staff to do the job right. Drop shipping is an asset to any business.

Drop Shipping Costs

The cost of Drop Shipping is determined by the Drop Shipper. It is very important for you to know the cost of Drop Shipping before you start Drop Shipping. You need to thoroughly research and look for companies that offer Drop Shipping service. Some wholesale companies as you no doubt know will not Drop Ship for you. There are others who will Drop Ship for an additional fee. It will enhance your bottom-line if you find a company who'll Drop Ship at no cost other than shipping and the cost of the merchandise. Some companies will charge a small membership fee at the beginning nevertheless this membership fee will be given back to you after you have made a certain number of purchases.

If you sign up with a company that charges a monthly fee you could end up giving away your profit for a month or two. You need to know all the cost of Drop Shipping so you can accurately calculate your profit. Be sure you get an itemized list of expenses from your Drop Shipper. You need to know the cost of the item, the charge for shipping, and taxes if any. Be reminded that some states charged an additional tax on purchases. If you are paying a monthly fee to a Drop Shipper you have to also prorate that fee into the total cost.

Remember there are always scams lurking to take advantage of beginners and others in any situation. You can always check with the Better Business Bureau to see if there have been complaints about the business dealings of any one of the Drop Shippers you find. Check with your Drop Shipper also to see how your account will be calculated. It is important to know whether you will be charged piece by piece or whether you will be charged on a monthly time table. Find out if the company accepts returns or what the return policy is.

If the company does not accept returns, then you may have to factor into your records a loss for that month. So that you will be able to adequately determine the cost for Drop Shipping, get all this information in writing before you start working with a company. Drop shipping can be a very efficient way to start a business it can enhance the bottom-line of any business but you need to know all the facts up front before you start. Even more so you need to let your customers know the return policy because eventually this can define your bottom-line.

Don't forget to get the company's policy for damage merchandise. Some companies will accept returns on damage merchandise and some companies will not accept returns on damage merchandise. Wholesalers that Drop Ship sometimes are reluctant to accept merchandise that has been opened and damage. So make sure you get in writing the policy the company will adhere to for damage merchandise that has been opened. Damage merchandise that the company will not accept as a return will be part of your Drop Shipping cost on the bottom.

How to Drop Ship

Have you ever been driving down the road and seen a bunch of large warehouse looking buildings Perhaps this is the industrial section of your community. More than likely these buildings that you see are used by drop shippers and other companies. These building are not opened to the general public for the most part. They house wholesale merchandise that is ordered by retail businesses for retail sales.

These buildings are scattered all over and they fill Drop Ship orders. The first thing you must do is to find a company that will drop ship for you. Find out what the guidelines for the company are before you agree to do business with them. Once you have decided which company you are going to use and the merchandise you plan to sell you are ready to pick the venue you plan to use to get customers. Drop shipping is very easy and convenient.

Most businesses that use this method of delivery seem to be very pleased. After you have collected the money for the merchandise from the customer, send the wholesale cost of the merchandise to your Drop Shipper; along with the money send the information as specified by the guidelines from the company. The drop shipper will then send the merchandise directly to the customer. That is all there is to. It is a very simple process; once you have worked with the company and established guidelines that you will adhere to in the processing of each order. If you don't already know how to Drop Ship you will find it a very easy process, and a convenient way to get merchandise to your customers. When you begin to get orders you will find that it is of uttermost importance that you keep good records of all transactions. You will need to keep a record of all orders if you have a copy machine it is advisable that you make a copy of all of your orders. Of course you will have a copy on your computer but sometimes as we know computers go down and you need a backup copy so keep a hard copy or paper copy of all orders. Organize your files in alphabetical order or what ever way you choose. For your Drop Shipping records, you need to keep them in a file cabinet for future references.

Make sure these files are accessible so if you have a drop ship inquiry from a customer you can quickly and efficiently retrieve the file. Many times a customer will e-mail you concerning a drop ship order that has not arrived. Check with your drop ship provider before returning a call or an e-mail. If an order that you Drop Ship is damaged, it is better to satisfy that customer if it all possible to the customer's satisfaction. In other words take the loss and keep the customer. In the long run drop shipping can be fun and rewarding. Keep an eye out for new merchandise that you can drop ship. You just may want to increase your business by adding another drop ship company to your list. Keep abreast of the market so you will know the hot items on the market. Find a supplier and add to your drop ship inventory.

Locate Drop Shippers

Make no mistake about it Drop Shippers are plentiful. There are several sources for finding names and addresses and phone numbers full Drop Shippers. Perhaps the number one place to look is the Internet. You are sure to pull up an abundance of names, all of which want your business.

If for one reason you do not find what you are looking for, you can still use the public library go to the business section and you are sure to find any number of bound directories that will lead you to Drop Shippers of your choice. Your local telephone director he may lend a helping hand to you with a local source. If so you may want to call them by telephone first, because in most Drop Shippers are not open to the public.

After all these are wholesale venues and they do not have display space. Bookstores will offer you a quick glance at some of the directors. They are bookstores that will allow you to sit and look through any book that is available in the store. And the same bookstores have a wide range of magazines available that will give you a chance to look at trade magazines. These magazines will list a number of drop shippers, giving addresses telephone numbers and all the information you need to get in contact with Drop Shippers. When you have contacted a few of these Drop Shippers you will begin to get mail and telephone calls from other Drop Shippers and other businesses. It seems that your name is put on a mailing list immediately after you have made contact with one or more of these Drop Shippers.

You will begin to get mailing lists and other pieces of mail from all kinds of Drop Shippers. There is no shortage of

Drop Shippers but make sure that you do a thorough and comprehensive search so that you will find the Drop Shippers with whom you will enjoy doing business. You will also receive wholesale list in the mail. Some of these companies will Drop Ship but be careful because some will just send you wholesale merchandise. It is important that you find Drop Shippers who will send single or small quantity orders. Since all Drop Shippers will not fit into your scheme of things make sure you know the policies is and guidelines of each company. Don't hesitate to call and asked the company questions if you do not see answers in the catalogs and other literature that you may have on hand.

Prepare an index listing of the names and other pertinent information of all Drop Shippers with whom you may do business. Let this be a flexible index so that you can add and delete Drop Shippers at will. Most of the Drop Ship companies are customer friendly because they are looking also to increase their bottom line. Drop Shippers are a major asset to small companies and help out in many ways. Drops shippers save small businesses in gas and time. If it were not for Drop Shippers you would have to factor in the cost of gas, maintenance and the wear and tear on your vehicle.

Novelties Wholesale

Novelties generate a nice income when bought for resale. Novelties are used for special occasions, birthday's, anniversary's, baby showers etc. The Novelty Wholesale Company is a family owned and operated business. The Company sells only the hottest Novelties and General Merchandise in the USA and around the World. The Company makes it real simple and easy to shop. Their policy is the more that you buy the more that you save. The wholesaler allows you to buy one item or sample or single units as well as buying in bulk.

Novelty Wholesalers supply many retailers, jobbers, wholesalers and the general consumer with their products. The family takes great pride in providing you with quality merchandise and fast, courteous service. Novelties Wholesale offers drop shop for you free of charge. There is no service fee. It is easy to join and there is no charge to be a member. This is how it works:

- ❖ It is free to join
- ❖ It is your own Business
- ❖ No product inventory
- ❖ You sell NW products on EBAY and online Auction Portals, Websites and NW drop ships for you.
- ❖ NW will ship worldwide
- ❖ NW provides you with the data, pictures and pricing to get started
- ❖ You get 25% of every sale.
- ❖ You only have to spend the time to set up your online store or EBAY Store and pay the Store Listing Fees and Seller Fees. NW wants to make it as easy for you as possible so they provide you with free listing tool. Also, be updated real-time when

any new items by subscribing to this RSS reader. Subscribe to the feed on eBay user id SURPLUS.

- ❖ NW is growing at an incredible rate giving you the opportunity to grow with us.
- ❖ The more items you put on your eBay Store, the more you will sell.
- ❖ NW has approx 2000 items ready for you to list.
- ❖ You make the sale, you send us the order along with you is discounted payment and we do the rest.

There are many different categories and items to put on your website and a great chance to make a profit.

The following was an example of one type of online Novelty Business but there are many other possibilities available that you should checkout. One of the other stores that offer online storefront is the Dollar Shop. Currently people just love to shop for a dollar. It is already set up for you and when people buy from your account then you are paid. The Dollar Shop also offers you so many free pages where you can put your own items on display. You still have a cart and the customers pay via pay pal. I like this part about the Dollar Shop because you make 100% profit on your pages.

Today Novelties are most certainly enjoyed by every one of all ages. It is fun to decorate for parties or have special Novelty items around for those special Holidays like Christmas. It is yes a growing business, which you can see by all the dollar stores in and around your neighborhood.

The Best Place To Be

One of the most reliable sources that you can use is eBay to become a seller. The process to become a seller on eBay is very simple and there is no need to worry about the company or driving trade your way. The requirements to become a seller are provide a valid credit/debit card and bank account information. If you do not want to provide this information, you can become ID Verified. It is highly recommended that you sign up to be a part of Pay Pal. Pay Pal is a valuable program that permits you to accept buyer credit cards and electronic check payments online. Pay Pal is vital because it keeps both the buyer and seller safe online. Pay Pal is an optional requirement but highly recommended. It is very easy to sign up on Pay Pal you can sign up when you list your first item or when you complete your sell your item form.

When you become a part of eBay, you must fill in your sell your item form. The reason is to create your eBay listing. You must select the type of format you plan to use for your sells. Selling formats consists of the standard online auction format, setting a fixed price, using your own eBay Store, or listing a classified ad. For those who plan on opening an online business and using a drop shipper, it is advisable to open up your own eBay Store. It is very advisable for you to explore eBay ahead of time so that you can determine the category that best suits your products. Look for items that are as the one is you plan on selling or popular categories that many customers seem to visit. Then when you think that, you have discovered the best type of product for your listing and category check out the drop shippers. Find out the most reliable drop shipper that carries the product that you plan on selling. Make sure the drop shipper is giving you the best price and has a reputation for prompt delivery.

Write a title that is clear, complete and descriptive. A well-written title that consumers will find easily when using the search engine is the key to driving consumers to your web site. Do not mention your drop shipper unless they are offering free shipping through the company.

It is true that some drop shippers will offer free shipping for a certain amount of sales and this can be a good thing to help you build volume. One nice thing about eBay is that you can offer details to help your item sell faster in the item specific option.

Next eBay offers a section that you can use to write an item description. This is your chance to really describe your item be clear and complete. Try to be a little bit creative by giving information about the item such as the history or ratings if possible but most of all try to relate to the customer why they would want to buy the item. One of the nicest things about eBay is the fact that you can show off your item with pictures or create a catalog for customer convenience if you are using a drop shipper that offers several products. All that you need to do is just click web hosting to use your own hosting service. You may select the how long your listing is going to run and change the listing when the item is gone or if no one is offering to buy. You can also state how many of the items you have the starting price or reserve a set price. eBay is truly the "best of the best" for those of us who have little to no funds and rely on drop shippers.

How They Help The Business

The Aid & Trade Drop Shippers is the answer to all your drop-shipping needs. The reality about the growing number of individuals who plan to make trading online is that 90% fail. Success stories are far and few in between. This is not due to lack of hard work or a good business plan but many balk under the adverse and challenging realities of the competitive world. We believe the reason for this failure is lack of information. These business failed because they could not manage to locate genuine and legitimate wholesale and drop shipping companies or drop shippers supplying the kind of niche goods that actually generate not only high number of sales but extremely high profits.

Aid and Trade provides a directory of legitimate drop shippers. They are about dedication, hard work, research and providing legitimate drop shippers that you can depend on. A drop shipper is the key to your turnkey business. You need to be able to depend on someone in the know in order to be able to survive even in the small business of on line virtual store. There are millions of products and thousands of drop shippers available but in reality, you only need one good drop shipper that is reliable.

One of the biggest problems that every start up company has to face is the warehousing and storing products. Normally, it entails renting a small storage place, which adds to the budget. Storing is not the only issue, developing product inventories, maintaining stock availability etc. The drop shipper helps you to get rid of all these issues so that you can concentrate on marketing and sales.

The drop shipper does the research for products provide you with a list and a catalogues of available items at trade prices. You can utilize this information and sell any of the product anyway you wish.

The drop shipper fills your order and helps with the tracking to make sure the customer is satisfied. The drop shipper does the packing of the product and the delivery you no longer have to package items or go to the post office. The drop shipper holds the product for you so that is a saved expense. The drop shipper does many of the jobs that would take up your time and your budget. At this point, you are able to spend more time doing marketing and sales to expand your business.

Even though the drop shipper provides all these tasks for you saving you in everyway, he is invisible to all your customers for only your name and address is on the product. That is one of the nice things about using a drop shipper it helps you to maintain a good standard in business, which is vital in keeping the business.

Drop shipping works very easy as first you open an Internet Store, with a shopping cart and the ability to accept credit cards. Then you find a distributor who is willing to drop ship the product you want to sell. You will establish an account as a retailer with the distributor you choose. Then you will receive images and descriptions of the products you want to sell from the distributor, and post them on your internet Store. Customer surfs into your store loves your items and possibly buys $100 worth of your goods, you then take it from their credit card along with the shipping rate. At that point, you email the order to the distributor who in turns sends the product directly to your customer then he charges you the wholesale price of the product plus his shipping charge. Your customer is happy and tells a friend and then you get more orders. The drop shipper is happy and fills all the orders you can send his way.

The Directory

We all need a road map to find out how to get to where we are going or we stop along the way and ask for directions. The same applies to those who want to use drop shippers in order to start up a virtual store on the web. The problem for many is that fraud is abundant and knowing whom to trust is a serious problem. The idea of getting involved with someone who is not legitimate could ruin your reputation and cause you not to be able to conduct business as well as bankrupt you financially. The use of a "Directory" that is reliable can save you a lot of problems and anguish from the start.

Today with a growing number of individuals allured by the profit, making opportunities are try to make a living by using the internet from the comfort of their own home. According to the industry estimates about 90% who venture into this line of business balk under the adverse and challenging realities of this competitive medium. One of the primary reason there are more disappointments and less success is because of the inadequate and unreliable information. A Directory of drop shippers and products that are based on legitimate sources is vital to the business. Many individuals have a great business plan and sound commitment on the idea of being a wholesale drop shipper.

We wish to introduce you to Aid & Trade a well-established company that has proven to be genuine, reliable drop shippers, and wholesale drop ship products in UK, USA, Canada, and other regions of the world. Aid & Trade can be the answer to all the questions you have about doing business with the use of drop shippers. The following is for those who are interested in knowing about:

- Where the power sellers in eBay purchase their products is vital information.
- Already in business, need to increase your profit then let us suggest that you use a Directory to help you do just that.
- The Directory offered by Aid & Trade explains how to sell products on eBay, your own website or other online auctions.
- The way to earn a part time or even a full time income from the comfort of your own home is by using good reliable drop shippers.
- Do you need help to find legitimate drop shippers and wholesale drop ship products with huge profit margins?

"If your answer is yes to any of the above statements then you need to go to Aid & Trade."

The Directory that they offer provides you with all the necessary information and it is kept up dated on a daily basis. They also offer counselors to help you decide on products and drop shippers. Stopping to ask for help after you have already started your drop ship wholesale product business may cause you some significant problems. The use of a GP Tracker or Directory is the key to arriving quickly and safely. The use of a good Directory that keeps you informed and up to date is the key to your success in business! Just as we advise you to use legitimate drop shippers we also would like to add use a reliable Directory for accurate information. Aid and Trade offers you a good Directory but remember there are other companies who are reliable as well. That is why it is very important for you to check your resources before going into business. You should find out not only which one's are reliable but who also offer wholesale products with prompt drop shipping.

Wholesale Distributor

The understanding of what it is to be a wholesale distributor will help you to a better understanding of drop shipping. The sale of goods in quantity is usually for resale by a distributor to a retail merchant. A wholesale made by the manufacturer in a large scale without discrimination requires a distributor to make sales to the retailer in smaller quantities.

The idea of wholesale distributors has been a marketing tool for a very long time. Earlier companies like the Fuller Brush Company, Sears, Montgomery Wards and J.C. Penny's started the basis of wholesale distributors and especially the idea of drop shipping.

The idea of Wholesale Products is vastly growing on the internet and becoming one of the leading ways of owning your own business without having to have money, building, and product. The reason being that your online store is normally manufacturers are more than glad to give you a cut on the profit in order to get their product recognized by the public and sold. The idea being your virtual store can have a large inventory without buying one product and the merchandise delivered instantly without anyone from your company getting involved. The key to having a good wholesale business is to find a reputable affiliate program; most of all find a way to drive traffic and sales toward your virtual store. Remember that most programs do include drop shipping as a means to get the product to the customer but you should make sure that shipping is either free or charged to the customer.

We have now discovered that the wholesale business is the easiest, fastest, and least expensive business to get started on the web. Now you need to get your creative juices working and do some researching to find out what you want to do in the wholesale business. Remember that with little to no capitol the business that you are strictly looking for is where you are the stockless retailer and the manufacturer drop ships the goods to the client. You also need a good affiliate program that will accept credit cards and papal.

Next, let me suggest that you check into eBay, as this is one of the best companies on line today for those who want to make sales. It is not complicated to list merchandise to sell on eBay. It requires a computer, internet connection, and a means of producing digital images. After you have become an active seller then you can open up your own eBay store for as low as $5 a month. eBay accepts the necessary means you need such as charge cards and pay pal, which helps you in receiving payments.

The next important part of your business is to drive customers to your store. It is very important to enable you to make the sales needed to keep your store open. We suggest that you use Google's AdSense program as it allows Web sites to display relevant ads on their website. When a web visitor "clicks" on an ad, the Web publisher will earn a percentage of any ad revenue generated. Our suggestion is that you build content Web sites that attract visitors and hope they click frequently on the ads. These suggestions are great to help you get started with your wholesale business but remember one of the most costly things to your business can be shipping. That is why drop shipping is necessary in any online business. The use of a drop shipper will save you millions of dollars a year. The key to a good virtual store is not only product but also distribution by the use of a drop shipper.

When You Decide to Drop Ship

So you have decided to go in business for your self. Even more so you have decided to Drop Ship your items. Before you do, make sure that your Drop Ship Company can supply the items you have in mind. It is perhaps best to start out with a few items so that you can become familiar with the drop ship process.

Several years ago, only a few companies would Drop Ship for you. Today there are a large number of companies that will sell you merchandise and Drop Ship it for you. If you feel that this is the business for you, then you need to start looking for Drop Ship companies. Decide what you want to sell, and then look for all the companies that offer these items. Consider the Drop Ship policies along with the price of the merchandise. Then you can determine whether to Drop Ship the items you want to sell. On the other hand, you need to know how much you want to make from your Drop Ship business. That will help you to determine the number of items to sell and what kind of items to sell. Even more so when you think of drop shipping you need to know the demand and supply for items you are going to sell.

If the item is a hot item, and you have many orders, there is a possibility that your company may not be able to fill your customer orders. There's nothing worse then ordering something only to find out that it is out of stock. So if you decide to Drop Ship, check with your drop shipper and make sure the item is available. It may not be possible some times to check with your Drop Shipper so be prepared to deal in customer service in a customer friendly way if the item ordered is out of stock. Most of the time Drop Ship companies have an abundance of merchandise; sometimes however, an item becomes very popular overnight. When this happens the supply can not fill the demand. Usually the wait for merchandise is not long but sometimes it is, especially if it is during a holiday time such as Christmas. So be prepared to deal with back orders and to communicate with your customers about the Drop Ship concerns.

For those business people who do not have storefront, drop shipping is an avenue for selling. When you decide to Drop Ship, you do not have to worry about stocking a store. The drop shipper has a warehouse full of merchandise and that becomes your store. Some drop shippers will allow you to come to the warehouse and look at the merchandise on display. If you can afford to visit one of these Drop Ship merchandise display centers, you can then pick and choose items that you think will Drop Ship well and that will be popular among your potential customers.

Remember items that are breakable, can create many problems for you from your customers. When an item is Drop Shipped, and a customer tells you that he received the item broken it becomes necessary for you to replace that item. Some items Drop Ship better than others. So pick a few items to Drop Ship at first, see how it goes and added on to your collection gradually.

Who are Wholesale Drop Shippers?

Wholesale drop shippers have existed for years even before the internet opened up to the wide world. Product distribution explains drop shipping so let us check out what exactly product distribution is about. In the olden days drop shipping started out as a simple procedure of getting products to the consumer. The Ajax Manufacturing company made cleaning supplies as an example and that was all that they did. The individual entrepreneur approached the Ajax Manufacture about getting the cleaning supplies in large quantities with an over all savings. The Manufacturer was happy to accommodate, as they were not in the business of selling.

The distributor then approached several retail outlet stores and offered them Ajax cleaners at a very reasonable price. In turn, the retail outlet could mark up the product and sell it to his consumer. All involved from the Manufacturer to the distributor to the retail outlet made a profit. The consumer found the product they wanted at a price they felt was reasonable.

This simple equation will help explain the above scenario.

1. Ajax Manufacturing sold products to a distributor for $12.00 a case of 12. Cost to make was .50cts per can. (profit $6.00)

2. The distributor sold the case to retail outlets for $24.00 a case. (profit $12.00)

3. The Retail Outlet marked each can out at $$3.50 a can (profit $18.00)

4. At a regular store, the Ajax cleaning products sold out at $4.50 a can so the consumer saved $1.00.

The beauty behind drop shipping is that the distributor places the order to the Manufacturer who in turn drops ships to the Retailer; therefore, the distributor does not have to buy in advance nor keep a lot of stock on hand. The process is so simple that it is hard to loose money on this type of procedure.

The invention of the internet greatly increased the business of drop shipping to a very profitable at home business. The idea of distribution started at the beginning of time with the first cave dweller trading fire for wood. For it is said without wood the fire will not remain and with out fire there is no need for the wood to remain. It takes both in order to keep one warm.

There are two types of retailers the one stocks merchandise for resale and the other stocks no merchandise is a stockless retailer. You as a drop shipper become the stockless retailer. The first type of retailer must have money to stay in business because they need to buy the merchandise, have an adequate storage place, and a retail place for sales. The second retailer only needs a computer. The drop shipper retailer opens up an Internet Store, with a shopping cart and the ability to accept credit cards. Many good distributors are willing to accept your orders and ship to the designated customer. You are not the "drop shipper" The company who supplies the products to your customer for you is the "drop shipper" "You become a Stockless Retailer". Today there are many on line Stockless Retailers and Drop Shippers you must make sure that you are dealing with real people and companies in order to prevent any fraud towards yourself and your clients. Fraud is the biggest problem you face.

Who is the Drop Shipper

The drop shipping business is a global business that spreads across all businesses and continents. The Drop Shipper may be right around the corner from you in a large building with enough space to store a variety of merchandise. On the other hand the Drop Shipper may be on the other side of the world. If you place an order today for merchandise you may receive it from Japan, China or anywhere in the world.

The varied modes of good transportation today make it possible to ship items within a two to three day period from anywhere in the world. Because of the Drop Ship business more goods and services are available to people all around the world. The Drop Shipper has made it possible to get things at a faster pace. Therefore any business with the necessary resources can become a Drop Shipper. In order to be a Drop Shipper there are certain things you must have in place. There are four basic things needed to become a Drop Shipper. They are money, facilities, merchandise, and staff. Money is always top of any list of needs in business. If you don't have the money you may be able to find a means to get the money. You may want to consider borrowing the money from a bank.

A large number of businesses have to take out a loan to have start up money for such a large operation. Some businesses have to take out several loans in order to have enough money to get started. When you have the necessary collateral, and a good business plan, banks will usually help you with the monetary resources to start a Drop Ship business. In addition to money you need to find a suitable location with the necessary facilities to store large quantities of merchandise. Don't forget to factor in the office space. Distribution facilities are usually not lavishly furnished as other office space. After all Drop Ship facilities are not usually open to the general public. Therefore there is no need for lavish chairs to accommodate clientele. Therefore you will see plenty of storage and hauling equipment scattered about in these facilities. A Drop Shipper needs to have resources and contacts to get merchandise as cheap as possible in order to sell wholesale. The Drop Shipper will find it also necessary to travel abroad and make contacts with merchants to get goods to wholesale. A large number of products that Drop Shippers sell come from places like China, Japan, Taiwan and other countries abroad. Some drop shippers make two to three trips abroad each year to find merchandise to wholesale. Wholesale list are sent out to retailers to inform them of new merchandise when it becomes available. So any business that has these resources in place can become a Drop Shipper.

Some chain stores have a drop shipper to handle the distribution of merchandise to customers. The Drop Shipper is heavily used with catalog companies. Have you ever wondered why the address on the package delivered is not the same address you sent your order to? The Drop Shipper's address is not the same as the company's address. So who is a Drop Shipper? The Drop Shipper can be any business that has the necessary resources in place. There are many other details that have to be worked out such as staff, insurance, policies, guidelines and transportation. All major forms of transportation will work with a Drop Shipper and be glad to do business with the Drop Shipper.

Who Uses the Service

Just about every other business at one time or another uses the service of drop shippers. The service industry makes maximum use of drop shippers. Drop Shippers supply parts for servicing various kinds of equipment. Many customers who do their own repairs, order various parts that they need and have them sent directly to the home address. The electrical industries do a great deal of Drop Shipping to customers. From time to time when the remote control on your TV goes out it becomes necessary to order a remote control online and have it sent by a Drop Shipper directly to you.

Many parts in technology have to be ordered or Drop Ship because they are not sold locally the Drop Shipper is usually not a manufacturer of parts but a distributor of parts. It is not always the manufacturer that does the drop shipping. If there are no distributors for the item the manufacturer will sometimes Drop Ship. Department stores interact with each other from city to city and Drop Ship to their customers.

It is easy to go on line to a department store and place an order and have it sent to someone in another city. Even department stores have on line businesses that use Drop Shippers. Drop shippers are used by most retail stores and wholesales stores. Drop Shippers have warehouses scattered in all regions and parts of the country. Jobs are created by Drop Shippers in small towns and communities and may be the primary source of income for that particular community. Usually in these small communities the labor force is abundant and there is no shortage of help at minimum wages. Many of the online stores distribute merchandise to these small communities to be distributed throughout the region. This cuts down on the expenses of the Drop Shippers by saving gas and time getting merchandise to customers. It is a great way to spread jobs throughout the country so those who want to work will have an opportunity to do so. Many immigrants work with these Drop Shippers on various shifts.

Even hospitals have used the services of Drop Shippers to deliver certain items to in-home patients. At one time automobile dealers picked up parts from a nearby warehouse when needed. Now when a customer orders certain parts they can have the parts sent straight to the customer. These automobile companies have Drop Shippers scattered across all regions of the country also. So the services of Drop Shippers or used by more than one type of industry. The use of a Drop Shipper depends on the service and the need that is required by the custom. Drop Shippers are a major part of the economy today. They are able to send merchandise to every crook and corner in the country. Drop Shippers have made it possible for you to order merchandise online one day and receive it the next day. This is because sometimes the Drop Shippers are located right around the corner from you. It is just a matter of loading the merchandise and bringing it to your door. It is not uncommon for customers to order today and receive tomorrow.

Work Together

The wholesale business has become a very active business while being a person who sells wholesale products you also need a delivery method. A good delivery method is the drop shipper who takes on the responsibility of delivery for you and maintains a large amount of stock for your business. We have mentioned many of the online wholesalers previously now I would like to mention one that we are all familiar.

Sam's Club a division of the Wal-Mart foundation provides for the business member the capability of having an online business.

The business member has many opportunities with Sam's Club to set up and maintain an online storefront. Sam's Club has the following opportunities:

- ✓ A five page website
- ✓ Industry templates to get you started
- ✓ Everything you need to get your business online and it is all complimentary!
- ✓ Domain Name
- ✓ Complete Business E-mail
- ✓ Maps and driving directions for your customer
- ✓ Weather reports right on the site
- ✓ Image Gallery
- ✓ The website is self edit
- ✓ Customer database Capability
- ✓ Event Calendar
- ✓ Polls and surveys
- ✓ Shopping Cart
- ✓ Tax and shipping Calculator
- ✓ Inventory Management

Sam's Club provides the best example of the uniting of wholesale and drop ship method to have your online business. Sam's Club makes it fast, easy, and affordable.

Oriental Trading Company, which began many years ago, started with the catalog order system. OTC provided many different novelty items that you could buy for resale and have shipped by a drop shipper. A pioneer in the wholesale and drop ship business OTC has lasted a long time and offers products at great prices. They also offer you the ability to be an affiliate and earn money by having your own website.

The combining of wholesale products with drop shipping has helped increase the retail business very much. The idea of having someone holding millions of products just for you and that you do not have to pay for him or her but can sell him or her and make a profit have been a boom.

The best method to combining the two procedures is by use of a directory. We all need a road map at times to find our way. It is very helpful to have a good directory so that you will know whom to use and how. The wholesalers catalog is very helpful in providing you with the names of wholesalers, manufacturers, and drop shippers. The Wholesalers catalog provides onetime special deals, closeouts, liquidations, below wholesale prices, including pallet loads and even truck loads from around the internet. You can buy in quantity or buy one product at the time. This is great for those who sell on eBay. Just browse through the categories or use search to see for yourself the endless possibilities. The Wholesale Catalog Company has spent many hours and had their representative's travel everywhere to put together this catalog just for you. The

Wholesalers catalog constantly adds so that you are up to date on products and drop shippers.

Who Are The Best

We have used some different terminology to explain the drop ship business. In the drop ship business, it is important to know who is who and what is what. Let us start in the beginning with the wholesalers. Many wholesalers are manufacturing companies that make a product out of their factory. They do not deal with sales or advertisement because this would indeed cause the cost of the product to be higher. The idea behind being a wholesaler is to make a good product cheap enough to reap a profit. The problem now is we have thousands of widgets but no customers. What must the wholesaler do?

Let us introduce the wholesaler to the distributor and his importance in getting the product to market. The distributor usually contracts with the wholesaler to buy his widgets at a reasonable price but still profitable to the wholesaler. The distributor then proceeds to either go out and find retail outlets that he can convenience to stock the product for resale or the distributor determines that he would be best suited to running his own online business. The distributor now becomes the retailer without physical property. The distributor must rely on the wholesaler entirely to maintain his online business.

Next, the distributor who is now the retailer must locate a reliable wholesaler to provide him product and shipping. That is where the drop ship business has spread so widely. The Worldwide Brands OneSource Product offers the best Wholesale and Drop-ship Directory with name brands at the absolute lowest prices. There are of course many other Directories for the wholesaler but most wholesalers find that it is best to be with a company that maintains a complete and up to date database.

Worldwide Brands lists genuine and brand new products only. Other directories on the internet have offered inferior quality goods that are copies or fakes. Products like this look good and you will probably get something on the bids but the price is always better when the product is genuine Sony for instance.

There are other advantages for those of us who live in the western world, as many of the companies listed will offer you low prices on a minimal order levels. For you the retailer this will save money, as you will not have to shell out exorbitant amounts of money to purchase initial stock. One of the great things by using a Directory from a reputable company like Worldwide Brands is that they insist that all distributors on the wholesale list offer a secure method of payment. The new person in drop ship business should use this directory for safety and convenience. You can of course use your own credit card or Pay pal, which offers greater levels of security.

The company started by people like you and I in order to help weed out the frauds and find the best products for less money helps all of us to maintain our business thus Worldwide Brands was born. Worldwide Brands is now a powerful company.

Wholesale Products Drop Shipped

Wholesalers are open to Drop Shipping whatever the public demands. The general public or the consumer determines what the retailer sells. Consequently, wholesale products are Drop Ship based on consumer demands. There is a wide array of products on the market today. Most wholesale products that are Drop Shipped are ordered online. A large number of homes today have access to the Internet. Many senior citizen homes have equipped their facilities with computers so seniors can shop online. A surprising number of seniors order items things from retailers online and these items are Drop Shipped to them. The wholesale products that are Drop Shipped are items that have been requested by individuals on line or from a catalog. There are dealers who will Drop Ship wholesale products in small quantities and in large quantities. Everything has to do with the bottom-line when you are in business.

Some dealers find it more profitable to Drop Ship wholesale products than to sell the traditional wholesale way. While there are others wholesalers who will not Drop Ship so it depends on the operation of the business. Wholesalers are the supplier of goods to the regular retail stores also. Some Drop Shippers do not sell goods locally but sell only online. More than likely these are the Drop Shippers who sell wholesale products. Drop Shipping wholesale products are a fast, quick and easy way to get products to a customer.

Selling wholesale products in small quantities and Drop Shipping these items is a very profitable and popular business. Some of the people who are in the wholesale business like working as a Drop Shipper instead of dealing directly with the public. These dealers enjoy moving volumes of merchandise at a time and working away from the hustle and bustle of retail businesses. It sometimes depends on what kind of staff and the organization of the business as to whether a wholesaler will Drop Ship wholesale products.

There are some wholesalers who will not Drop Ship wholesale products but will deliver wholesale products by the truckloads to department stores, boutiques and specialty shops. These are the dealers who enjoy moving large quantities of merchandise in one scoop. All kinds of merchandise can be Drop Ship, but when you think of Drop Shipping wholesale products you think of small items and midsize items. Usually wholesale Drop Shipping involves a single order of two to three items shipped to one individual. Nevertheless there is no limit on the number of items that can be Drop Ship to an individual. Most of the time Drop Shipping of wholesale products is done for small companies that do not have the facility and resources for larger operations. There are some wholesale Drop Ship companies who will Drop Ship to members only. So it may become necessary that you sign up and give pertinent information before you are allowed to do business with the company. Not all prices are wholesale prices.

So be sure to check out every facet of the company before signing up and making a purchase. You have to look at your bottom-line to make sure that you will have a profitable experience.

Use a Wholesale Shipper

A wholesale shipper is the ideal way to start a business with little to no funds. The wholesale shipper offers convenience, keeps the merchandise stored, and makes delivery as you request it. Depending on how hard and how much you wish to expand your business you can determine which wholesale shipper will best suit your needs.

In order to understand the role of the wholesale shipper we first need to understand product distribution. First, the product has to be assembled and packaged for resale that is where the Manufacturer starts everything going. The Manufacturer does not advertise or try selling the product because they are too busy making the product. Therefore, the wholesale shipper bargains with the Manufacturer to buy the product either in bulk or piece by piece. The wholesale shipper also bargains with the Manufacturer concerning the shipping, as this is a vital part of how the product is marked up. Now you the retailer look for a good distributor and wholesale shipper because in most cases they are both the same. After you make a buying agreement with the wholesale shipper then you are ready as the retailer to set up shop. You have your choice of a regular brick and mortar store or a virtual online store.

Today many people elect to have a website and to have an online store. The main reason being with the use of a wholesale shipper and the ability to do drop shipments a person can start a business with practically no money or a bit of pocket change. The wholesale shipper manages the buying of products, the storing, the shipping and even furnishing you with a website in some cases. The opportunity that you now have is unlimited it only takes a lot of hard work. Many business people are finding that being able to stay at home earn a sizeable income is more to their liking than going to work everyday. The wholesale shipper does the majority of the work while you as the retailer earn most of the profits.

In order for you to be able, to make it all come together you need a wholesaler's directory. The number one Wholesale Directory is ONESOURCE by World Wide Brands. ONESOURCE gives you all the advantages that you would need to set up your business and keep it going making a substantial profit. They offer drop ship, light and bulk products, along with having over 9000+ suppliers. World Wide Brands has over three million products and import wholesale supplier's products. The World Wide Brands is the "BEST" Wholesale and Drop-Ship Directory with Name Brands at the absolute lowest prices! The company offers quality supplies with secure purchasing.

If you have ever wondered how people make a lot of money on eBay then wonder no more. World Wide Brands is one of the most used companies by eBay sellers. EBay sellers have the option of just buying a single item for auction or buying in bulk for their virtual store. Since World Wide Brands is taking care of your order then all you are required to do is the billing and collecting of the money. They normally ship after you have received payment from your customer. World Wide Brand also only uses wholesale shippers to save both you and your customers.

There are of course other Directories available on line for you to check out. It would be a good thing for you to do just that and pay close attention to the wholesale shipping industry. The wholesale shipping program offered by different distributors may vary in that some only ship in bulk while others will ship both bulk and individual products. The wholesale shipper is the key to a good business that will last.

Use Drop Ship Products

Today we have the whole wide world at our finger tips to select products that we want to have drop shipped to the consumers. Major brands offer their products for an online virtual storefront hosting the website for you and providing the drop shipping. The quest is not so much selecting a product but selecting "the" product. First take a look at the company that you plan to use for some of the following characterizes:

- Look at the overall ranking of this drop ship company in comparison to other reliable companies.
- You should be able to buy directly from the drop shipper at drop ship prices.
- Depending on the specific product, can you get a free trial or a demo?
- You should be able to access the product without too much difficulty.
- The company should be a Member of the BBB in good standing.
- You should be able to get the BBB Status and Rating information.
- Does this company offer a sound support desk and support forum.
- Are you able to get into a support knowledge base for quick answers?
- You should be able to contact the drop shipper directly.
- The drop shipper should be upfront about what percentage the product is marked up.
- A very important part of the product business line is that the drop shipper ships with your name and address.

- Remember if you use your credit card, you will pay out more but if you can use Papal, it will save both you and your customer.
- The affiliate program is a needed tool that will increase your business.
- Information is the key to most all-successful business so make sure they do offer some educational tools.
- Finally find out how long they have been in business and how reliable are they.

Now that you have some good information on what to look for when you are trying to set up your drop shipper to supply you with products let us take a look at some of the best noted companies. The following companies can be found on different search engines.

The first drop ship company that offers all the things one needs to be successful is www.usellcorp.com . Usellcorp has a full review and offers all of the above-mentioned qualifications. They also have a huge amount of merchandise to offer you. Usell Corp has been in business since 1995 so they have been around long enough to formulate a good reputation.

The second recommended drop ship company with full review is www.worldwidebrands.com This Company offers name brand items at wholesale prices. They ship from all around the world so if you like to diversify and use a variety of goods this would be a great company for you. Worldwide Brands has been in business since 1999 an outstanding member of the BBB, which is an excellent place for you to begin your inquiries.

The third formable company is www.truedrop shippers.com, which carries an excellent record as well. Just like the other companies, you can check out their policies and their record before you decide to use one of them. Many times these companies will send you a catalog or have one available for you to access on line. You should most certainly check different web sites to find out what are the best products with a good turn over and a great profit margin. True Drop shippers is one of the newer companies beginning in 2003 but have so far showed their importance in the market place. There are other companies that are acceptable but the review is not quite as high as the above three major companies. It is not to say that they would not fit your needs and are worth your while to check them out. Let us recommend to you companies like Doba, DSDI, Drop ship Design, and Mega Goods for they too have a good reputation.

The product or products you decide to sell are the utmost importance along with having a very good drop shipper that keeps the commitments of all the orders. It takes both in order to maintain your business successfully.

Why use Drop Shipping

In today's world, many people try to operate a profitable business by using the internet. It is much simpler to have a virtual storefront than to have a brick and mortar store. In addition, it is much cheaper to operate. One of the major reasons that the cost of operation is minimal is due to the process known as drop shipping.

Drop shipping seems to be a magical way of getting merchandise, selling the merchandise, delivering the merchandise, while not visibly seeing the merchandise. This may sound a bit complicated but actually, it is very simple. To use an example let us use the Dutch Maid Manufacturer of cleansers. Dutch Maid makes a lot of product but they are not in the business to sell or distribute the product. The next group let us introduce is Mr. Distributor who is the person who goes to the Dutch Maid Manufacturer and contracts to buy the product by the case at a dollar a can or $12 a case. The Manufacturer declares that it cost him .50 cents a can to make, so there is a $6 a case profit. The Manufacturer is happy because he has profited without having to try to sell or advertise which has greatly saved on the company's profit margin.

Let us take this a step forward, as Mr. Distributor now needs to sell the product in one of two ways, which are by soliciting retail stores and having them agree to buy the product or by opening up a website where Mr. Distributor can take orders and sell on line. In both cases, the process of drop shipping plays a vital part in Mr. Distributor business. First Mr. Distributor now has a good product for resale but does not have to keep it stored nor does he have to open up a storefront to display the product. He is using the drop shipping method simply put the retail stores order from him and he sends the order to the Dutch Maid

Manufacturer who sends the product to the customer. This is why the use of drop shipping is the best way to run a business without too much investment.

This sounds like a sure fire way to make money without loosing a truly profit making opportunity. Unfortunately, success stories are rare as those who venture into this line of business balk under the adverse and challenging realities of the competitive medium. The primary reason for these unfortunate cases is not in the business plan or the lack of commitment on the part of those behind the idea, but rather it is inadequate and unreliable information. Most entrepreneurs fail because they did not locate genuine and legitimate wholesale and drop shipping companies. The other reason being the drop shippers is not supplying the kind of niche goods that actually generate not only high number of sales but extremely high profits as well. The use of a good drop shipper is one of the most vital aspects of a distributors business.

Use the Drop Ship Method

The best answer to that are money, time, and success. Yes, the drop ship method saves the retailer lots of money.

- ✓ The seller saves by not having to pay for a storage space.
- ✓ The seller saves by not having to have a bulk of product on hand that is not selling.
- ✓ The seller saves because he no longer has the expense of packaging and shipping the product.
- ✓ The seller saves money by not having a large payroll. The seller does not need a staff the drop ship method takes care of that.
- ✓ The retailer saves valuable time so that he can do things that are more important.
- ✓ The retailer does not have to do the research work to find products and shippers in order to meet quota.
- ✓ The retailer saves time by not having to package and ship the product.
- ✓ The retailer saves time by not having to drive to work and back home again.
- ✓ The retailer actually saves money and time by having a virtual storefront.

The drop ship method has helped many people to have a very good income without having to make a large of investment cash, store products, and finding the right products for sales. The use of a drop shipper is truly necessary for this kind of business.

The drop ship method is so simple that anyone can do it if with the desire and the proper information. It is not complicated and most companies provide advisors to help you so that when you first start up you will know what to do to expect. Many companies have their own sites and offer a forum so they can speak one to another and get ideas. The online advisors can also help to solve any problem you might be having. It is not easy to get free advice when you are in business. It is easy to get fraudulent information loosing a lot of money and not ever seeing any returns. That is why the drop ship method is so popular it helps resolve many issues in an honest manner.

The OneSource Directory offers you connection to over 9000 suppliers and over three million products. The company also does the Import wholesale supplier business so that is something you do not need to worry about but you can benefit from the wholesale products. The "HOT" products to sell online are provided for your benefit so that you can decide to sell them or not.

The best things are that you are informed about with EBAY what is selling now and how it is going. As we, all know EBAY is one of the leading online companies people use to sell and buy products. The company offers auctions, classified sales and a storefront that you can use and well known by everyone worldwide. Many people do sell on EBAY and many people go to EBAY to buy a product. The ease of using EBAY has caused many people to quit the mainstream of work and stay at home working from their home office.

www.ingramcontent.com/pod-product-compliance
Lightning Source LLC
Chambersburg PA
CBHW051249170526
45165CB00004B/1640

* 9 7 8 1 4 8 2 0 6 5 0 6 0 *